In the Creole Twilight

In the Creole Twilight

Poems and Songs from Louisiana Folklore

JOSHUA CLEGG CAFFERY

LOUISIANA STATE UNIVERSITY PRESS

BATON ROUGE

Published by Louisiana State University Press
lsupress.org

Louisiana Paperback Edition, 2024

Designer: Michelle A. Neustrom
Typeface: Adobe Jenson Pro

Cover illustration: Detail from *Swallow and Crow,* by Claire Caffery.
All illustrations are by Claire Caffery and are reproduced by permission
of the illustrator.

LIBRARY OF CONGRESS CATALOGING-IN-PUBLICATION DATA

Caffery, Joshua Clegg.
    [Poems. Selections]
    In the Creole twilight : poems and songs from Louisiana folklore /
Joshua Clegg Caffery.
        pages ; cm
    ISBN 978-0-8071-6154-8 (hardcover) — ISBN 978-0-8071-6155-5
(pdf) — ISBN 978-0-8071-6156-2 (epub) — ISBN 978-0-8071-8289-5
(paperback) 1. Folklore—Louisiana—Poetry. 2. Folk music—Louisi-
ana. 3. Louisiana—Poetry. I. Title.
    PS3603.A3775A6 2015
    811'.6—dc23

                                            2015006257

To
Jean Arceneaux
and
Carrington Cabell Tutwiler III

La terre nourrit tout,
Les sages et les fous.
 —anonymous song

Contents

Author's Note

I began thinking about this work while in the midst of a two-year
period during which I did little but transcribe and research songs
recorded from the oral tradition of south-central Louisiana. As
an aspiring scholar with an antiquarian bent, I was interested in
the nature and origin of these materials. But I was also inspired,
as a writer of songs and poems myself, to turn them over in my
mind and to rework them into my own words and to thread them
around my own life in new ways. During a year-long fellowship in
the Library of Congress's Thomas Jefferson Building, after or before
a day of research and academic treasure-hunting, I had the chance
to do just that, and I wrote most of these poems in the light that
filters down through the great dome of the library's main reading
room. The poems in this slender book, therefore, are all invocations
or evocations of matters drawn from Louisiana folklore. Some
are fairly direct reworkings of song plots, while others grow out of
syllabic structures and rhyme schemes or simply arresting images or
characters. In the notes at the end, I've offered some brief thoughts
on the old stories and my own efforts to bring an echo of them into
the present.

In the Creole Twilight

Prologue

You say you'd have the secret of the songs in this swamp. There are practically none. Are there any secrets in the patterns cast by a cypress against the sky in Lost Lake?

Patterns are no secrets, but I'll tell you about one, one that stretches like a branch across the sun, that swims like the sunfish through the trunks, that swoops like the owl from perch to perch, that moves through the brambles with a lightning lurch: Fido dies. If some logic dwells in the riddle here before us, or if there is a rhythm or a secret in disguise, it all begins with this: Fido dies. It is never a surprise.

If you've heard of Joe Féraille, you know that by the time you've heard, a train will have come by, killing Fido on the tracks. Please, do not ask me why. Concentrate upon this fact: Fido dies.

Now, Casey Jones took Fido's hide and fashioned gloves for his new bride; he crushed a redbug's guts and sprinkled them inside. And what are those bright baubles, you ask, dangling on her necklace and glittering in the light? A word to the wise: those are Fido's eyes. Fido always dies.

Therefore, before we begin, let me reassure you that I'll never tell you lies. I cannot explain the leafless words unfolding in these twilit skies. But one thing that I do know (and that I truly must emphasize): in the creole twilight, Fido always dies.

A Letter to Pierre Grouillet

I remember our wedding day, Pierre,
    I was watching from the window in Mother's room
    while your friends chased chickens through the coop.
The fat one, the butcher, banged on the door,
    singing, "Peasant, come down
    from the second floor."

Outside, Théogene was laughing and drunk,
    shooting at a rooster with a rusty gun.
I was hiding in Mother's wicker chest
    when you found me, tearing my vest
    as you yanked me up.
A packet of tobacco and a pat on the back—
Father forgave you just like that.

They tied me in ribbons and spun me around
    (white, red, and yellow as a candy cane),
    rolling over the muddy ground
    in an ox-drawn hack down the country lane.
While you wrestled with Doucet down in the ditch,
    I wrestled the ribbons off of my hips,
    and the only one who saw me cry
    was the handsome fiddler with the hazel eyes.
The whole way home, he held my gaze,
    walking backward while he led the parade.

Now I'm sitting on the banks of the Tennessee,
    and that fiddler man sleeps close by me,
    bound for Baltimore and Aunt Eulalie.
They said you were a carpenter, a solid trade,
    but I've cast in the current the cross you made,
    whittled from cypress, soft and red.
    I never once wore it around my head.

The Feufollet of Irish Bend

Come all you fine young children,
Those who are wise and willing to hear.
Those who are brave will all gather near,
And all are advised now to listen.
It's a tale that might scare you, I fear,
So sit close to your cousin or friend.
A tale of the marsh and the harshest of years
Along the old Irish Bend.
Along this bend in the bayou, my dears,
Along the old Irish Bend.

When your grandfather's grandfather came to the Bend,
He was a young pioneer—
He and two brothers, all brave pioneers.
They settled the forsaken swampland.
The youngest was wild—that was clear.
He rambled around with a jug in his hand
And a scraggly, untidy beard.
He took a young bride at the Indian post,
Discarded her later that year.

A baby was born to the Indian girl,
But no chapel or church-house was near.
No priest or prelate was near.
No one to baptize the infantile spirit.
It died in a fever that year.
No god above them could hear it
When it died, unbaptized, that year.
No angel on high could come near it,
When it died from a fever that year.

After the death of this beautiful child,
Strange tales they started to hear,

Strange stories that filled them with fear,
Related by travelers come through the wild
Of shimmering lights that would oddly appear
In the marshes or swampland nearby.
The flickering fires would fade then appear,
Leading a traveler astray.
Strange lights on the road that led here.

For they say that the souls of dead children,
Unblessed by the Lord will appear
(When you are alone will appear)
As lights in the marshes unbidden,
Guiding you into the mere,
Far from the path you had ridden,
Far from the roadways, I hear.
The vengeful ghosts of dead children,
Barred from the heavenly sphere.

And they say that the only known cure
Is a knife with the blood of a steer,
The blood of a bloody black steer
Into a fencepost secured.
And so the youngest grabbed his blade
And stumbled out with a sneer.
Waving his knife, he yelled to no one,
"I'll finish this thing, do you hear?"
He yelled to the heavens and held up the knife.
"I'll finish this thing. Do you hear?"

They found him next morning face down
In the muck. He was dead, or so it appeared.
His throat had been cut ear to ear.
In a fencepost nearby, the dagger was plunged.
And that was the end of the youngest son.
They buried him later that year,

Buried him without a tear.
And they never heard tell of more lights on the road
Through the marsh on a midnight so clear.
And you'll hear no more tales of lights in the swamp.
They're all gone, or so it appears.

Saint Catherine and the Cherubim

Catherine was a Persian princess,
Imprisoned in a tower.
Her father was a jealous king
Who came by every hour

To see if she would pray,
To see if she would kneel.
In his hand there gleamed the hilt
Of a saber made of steel.

A week before, he'd seen her
Walking in the square,
Talking to a filthy Christian
With matted, unkempt hair.

In the tower's highest reaches,
Catherine was thrown.
Seven days she sat there,
Weeping, all alone.

"If I see you kneel or pray,
Or hail the god-man Christ,
I'll unsheath this saber
And behead you with one slice."

On the seventh evening,
He burst through the door.
On the wall a cross was scrawled.
She was sprawled across the floor.

Where once there were two windows,
Now he could see three.

"A third," she breathed, "For Jesus Christ,
And for the Trinity!"

And so he raised his shining saber
And began to bring it down,
But Catherine smiled and, pointing, said,
"Father, turn around."

And there he saw the Cherubim,
With flaming sword, divided face,
The same that guards the eastern side
Of Eden's shining gates.

Then the angel screamed,
A voice half bull, half bird.
A cry of pure terror
No living man has heard.

Backing up, he stumbled.
Backing up, he fell
And through the window plummeted
As the mouth of fiery hell

Opened far below,
Opened its smoldering maw.
His daughter's face in the window high
Was the last thing that he saw.

And the last thing that he heard
In the heavenly, hellish wind,
Was the angel sweetly screeching,
"All praise Saint Catherine."

Sans-Souci

Listen you all, I was born in the fall.
My mother is dead, a bachelor's my dad.
Here's what he said (scratching his head):
"I'll raise you in pleasure,
A life full of leisure.
The world is your toy, my joyful young boy."

When I was fourteen, that bachelor turned mean.
He sent me to school, where they called me a fool;
They made me learn cursive,
But I would just curse if
That silly schoolmistress
Accused me of mischief.

When I reached twenty-five, he found me a wife.
A dowry quite large, and I was in charge.
"How will you spend it, dear?
To whom will you lend it, dear?"
"Calm down," I said,
Patting her head.
"I'm in charge, dear. Now go back to bed."

Now sixty-five and barely alive;
Each little breath brings me closer to death.
One simple task is all that I ask:
When I am dead,
Put a jug at my head,
And sprinkle some wine on my grave.

Têche

Once I saw
    a speckled kingsnake
        chase a skink
            across your muddy stomach
      slither stealthily into the grass
sliding from side to side
      slightly shaking
        the sunny clover.
           One summer by the slip
                I sat for hours
            with a saltwater rod
          and a stinking shrimp
      stalking gars with stiff jaws.
Charles passed from the quarters
      stopped and sat in the shade
        sipped Coors and
          smiled as the gars
          slung the cork sideways
        advised patience
    for the swallowed hook.
Most of my days were spent
    beside your banks.
      Now in the city
          you coil inside me though
        as it was for priests of Israel
        you are sacred.
      Someday
when the sun
    cascades
      into the grass
        the skink will surrender,
And you will straighten into a staff.

The Ring and the Cormorant

One evening at the water's edge,
Isabelle observed a ship's approach,
A boat full of soldiers, thirty in all,
Alongside a bayou in March.

Someone was singing on the bow,
The youngest sailor of the crew.
A wisp of a beard and a grin,
And his voice—a melodious coo.

"I'd love to learn the song you sing,
So sweet and archaic it sounds.
Teach it to me. I'll give you my ring.
Stroll with me here on the ground."

"Embark with us now if you want this sweet song,
I'll teach you to sing like the swallow.
Climb on aboard, and you'll have my word.
No reason to wait for tomorrow."

But as she stepped on, her gleaming gold ring,
A gift from a fond old father,
Slipped from her finger, struck off the rail,
And plummeted into the water.

Stripping off shirt and boots and belt,
He plunged for it into the river.
A minute passed, and he surfaced for air,
No glittering ring to deliver.

The second plunge was much the same,
Though, weeping there on the deck,

She noticed a feather, greasy and black,
Uncurling from out of his neck.

The third plunge down, the bayou boiled,
And from the surface, with a shriek,
A water bird, a cormorant,
Flew up with the ring in its beak.

No swallow's coo, no gentle sound,
But a cormorant's ugly cry.
Black and wet, it circled around,
and flew off in the darkening sky.

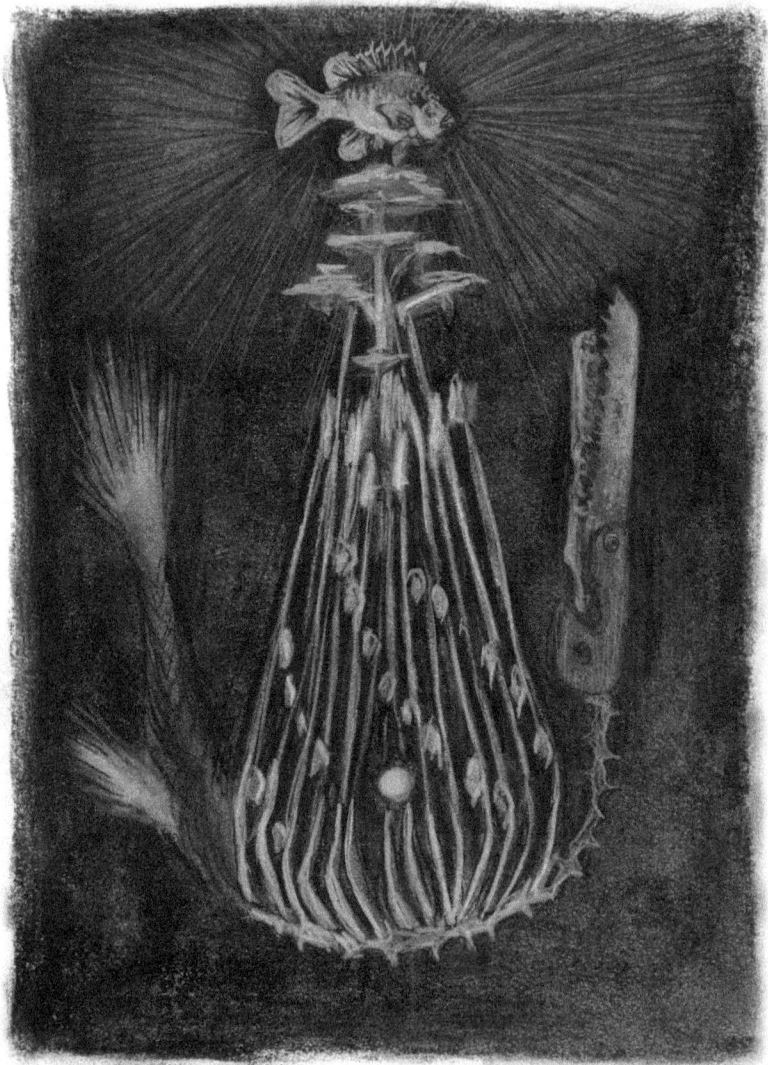

Sunfish and Loom

If you were a girl on the bayouside,
I'd embrace you and make you my darling bride.
I'd pay the right price,
I'd tell my mother twice,
If you were a girl on the bayouside.

If you were my suitor on the bayouside,
I'd be a cypress tall and high.
You'd trip in my roots
In your store-bought boots
If you were a suitor on the bayouside.

If you were a cypress tall and high,
I'd be a saw and I'd try
To slice at your knees
In the soft bayou breeze,
If you were a cypress tall and high.

If you were a saw with an iron blade,
I'd be a sunfish, and I'd swim away.
Your teeth would rust,
They'd turn to dust,
If you were a saw with an iron blade.

If you were a sunfish, glittering gold,
I'd be a garfish, slimy but bold.
In the bayou brown
I'd track you down,
If you were a sunfish, glittering gold.

If you were a garfish, slimy and green,
I'd be a microbe too small to be seen.
Your giant jaw would jut

And I'd hide in your gut,
If you were a garfish, slimy and green.

If you were a microbe infesting my tissue,
I would be happy just to be with you.
I could only rejoice
If you made such a choice,
If you were a microbe infesting my tissue.

If you were happy to be so infested,
I'd multiply quickly inside your flesh and
Leave you alone,
A pile of old bones,
If you were happy to be so infested.

I would be proud to be so consumed.
My bones would transform into an ivory loom.
I'd start over again,
I'd weave a new skin.
I'd be delighted to be so consumed.

The Wooden Leg

An old fool waving his hands
Hobbles around on a peg.
That's what you see, but don't be unkind;
Consider with a philosophic mind
All the joys that accrue to a wooden leg.

I'm like a child again, you see,
Carefree beneath a sky of blue,
Spending so little on socks,
Wasting so little on shoes.
Listen closely while I teach:
With a wooden leg, you need just one of each.

Once, when I hurt my leg,
The doctor made a hefty profit.
Now I head off for the lumberyard,
Put a dowel on my card,
And think practically nothing of it.

And when my wife becomes a shrew
And snaps or scolds for hours,
She finds no meek, pathetic mouse.
When I raise my leg aloft,
She beholds the master of the house.

And when the winter wind blows in
And icicles clutch the trees,
The woodpile may grow low,
But I have no pressing need
For a poker or a wheezing bellow.
My wooden leg will stir the coals,
And I'll remain a happy fellow.

The Flame and the Tower

There was a girl of just fifteen,
With hair of gold and eyes of green.
Her father was a jealous sort,
Red of eye and black of heart.

She loved a boy named Amédée
With hair of gold and eyes of gray.
He rode a horse with dappled skin
Whose mane flowed wildly in the wind.

Her father hated Amédée,
Despised his eyes of placid gray.
He built a tower hard and high,
Black and cold against the sky.

Cutting off her golden hair,
There he hid his daughter fair.
Around the tower, dark and steep,
He built a moat both wide and deep.

"You may not cross this, Amédée,
With your eyes of gentle gray.
You may not cross this icy moat
Upon your horse of dappled coat."

That night the girl of just fifteen
Received a message in a dream:
In your window, light a flame,
A single flame to guide his way.

And so she lit a flaming candle,
Placed it gently in the window.

Then she slept and dreamt no more
Until the sunlight crossed her door.

Down below the sable keep,
She saw a sight that made her weep.
Two bodies floating in the moat
And one the horse of dappled coat.

And one the shape of Amédée,
Now shut those eyes of quiet gray.
"No," she wept, "it cannot be.
The dream I dreamt was false to me."

So she pierced a single vein,
And from above red droplets rained.
They struck the surface of the moat,
Awoke the horse of dappled coat,

Opened the eyes of Amédée,
Those startled eyes of silent gray.
And up he leapt onto his horse
And round the tower ran the course.

They spiraled upward, horse and man,
And Amédée held out his hand
For the girl of just fifteen,
With hair of gold and eyes of green.

And far above the icy moat,
She mounted that horse of dappled coat.
And as they quickly flew away,
She held on tight to Amédée.

The Loup-Garou

When I got rid of Joan,
I was living alone,
On the banks of brown Bayou Blue.
I saw it one night,
In the fluorescent dock light,
The creature called Loup-Garou.
The beast known as Loup-Garou.

Head of a wolf,
Arms of a man,
Teeth of a bat,
It started to stand.
It grimaced and growled
At the rising moon.

In a guttural howl,
In a horrible croon,
It wailed out its name
To the curd-colored moon:

    Loup-ga
    Loup-ga
    Loup-garou

    Loup-ga
    Loup-ga
    Loup-garou

To a barbaric beat,
It stomped its feet,
Filling its mouth with a fistful of meat.
As I bolted the door,
It howled once more.
I covered my ears and
Crouched on the floor.

That was then, this is now.
Joan took me back—I don't know how.
I sold my camp, and we live in town.

But on a full moon, I still hear the sound
I heard that night on Bayou Blue.
I still hear the Loup-Garou—

    Loup-ga
    Loup-ga
    Loup-garou

    Loup-ga
    Loup-ga
    Loup-garou.

When You Meet Two Friends

When you meet two friends,
In town or country lane,
Never pass between them
Or it will bring you shame.

When cutting fish to fry or stew,
To boil or to bake,
If you cut your finger,
Throw that fish away.

If you move from house to house
And plan to bring your cat,
Pass him through the window
Or risk a heart attack.

When you hear an owl screech
The first day of July,
Light a candle on the sill
Or someone close might die.

When Rooster cackles on the porch,
You'll see a long-lost friend,
When Rooster crows at midnight,
The fog will soon roll in.

If you stop to see a friend
And enter through the side,
Never leave through back or front
Or conflict will arise.

If you kill a frog
Or cause a poor toad pain,
Have an umbrella at hand,
For it will surely rain.

If fleas invade your house and home
And start to drive you mad,
Crumble ten pecan leaves
And spread beneath your bed.

If, strolling through the forest fair,
Poison ivy do you find,
Point it out and loudly shout,
"I curse you, evil vine!"

Never give a friend a knife
Without payment or receipt,
If you do, he'll turn on you,
And friend no longer be.

Never pass a baby boy
Through a window high,
Or he will be a lazy thief
Until the day he dies.

Pick up a pin from off the ground
When pointed at your feet.
If it's pointed elsewhere,
Make sure to let it be.

If your hair should break and fall,
Burn it right away,
Or a bird will make a nest from it
And your head will ache all day.

If a foul wart should sprout
Upon your hand or ear,
Take two matchsticks, break and burn them.
It will disappear.

If, walking down the road,
You should have to turn around,
Cross yourself from left to right
Before you travel on.

Big Bull, Little Horn

Big bull, little horn,
Shame that he was ever born.
Big chair, little man,
Oyster in a frying pan.
Bachelor's house, funny smell,
Wife will never come to dwell.
Fancy cat, so dignified,
Hisses when the dog comes by.
Death, O Death, honest thief,
Rich and poor will both agree.
Big road, easy fight,
Little house, lasts all night.
"Will you? Will you?" asks the Favor,
"No, sir. No, sir. Maybe later."
Chickens crying in the barn,
Preacher man is on the lawn.
Funny thing, my enemy
Wears an overcoat like me.
Here's another funny thing:
When it rains, the bullfrog sings.
Gator garbed in scales and slime,
Hornet shouldn't waste his time.
Sleet or snow or wind or rain,
Never cross a funeral train,
And never wear your mourning dress
Till the dead are laid to rest.

Gabriel and Madeline

Gabriel and Madeline make a funny pair.
Gabriel's my godfather,
He rides a chocolate mare.
Madeline's my godmother.
Don't take her for a fool,
Although she gets around
On an old three-legged mule.

When I was christened, Gabriel
Showed up with Josephine.
She spit tobacco from the pew
And made the preacher scream.
Madeline grabbed her cuff
And hauled her down the aisle,
Threw her in the churchyard.
That made the preacher smile.

But Madeline, it must be said,
Is not a saint, I know.
They caught her kissing Uncle Adam
In the cotton rows.
Never one to be outdone,
To hide at home and grieve,
Gabriel got caught in the chicken coop,
Kissing Auntie Eve.

The Giantess Bride

My mother wed me to a giantess.
She scooped me up and off she stomped,
Over the levee and through the woods,
Deep into the wilds of Hog Island Swamp.

She lost me in her corn-shuck cot.
(Truthfully, I hid.) She lit a flame
To find me and the corn shuck caught—
Grilled me to a crisp.

Then she dipped me in a pail of milk,
Where I began to wail and cry
As "Precious Pet," her panther-cat,
Commenced to chewing on my thigh.

There is no moral to this tale, my friend.
And while it has been nice, you should go.
The dusk is creeping up the bank,
And my bride will soon be home.

Home from the Forest

I set out along the tree line.
A man was splitting timber.
He spoke, but what I understood
I hardly can remember.
"It's hard," he said, "it's hard.
In truth, there is no cure."
But this is what I thought I heard,
"You simply must endure."
At least that's what I thought he said,
And alone through the forest I fled.

I came across an owl hooting
In a sycamore by a silver stream.
He said to me in his manner of speaking,
"If you were a rat you would scream."
I shook my head and listened
For a low and comforting hoot,
But he swiveled his head, and he whispered,
"I'm coming after you."
Then screeching he flew for my head,
And alone through the forest I fled.

Finally I found a field full of wheat,
Where a reaper was peacefully reaping.
She remarked in her tongue, "I can't stand this heat;
The time will soon come for sleeping.
The time will soon come," she said, waving her scythe
And twirling with uncanny pace.
Her cowl slipped down. She started to writhe,
Revealing a skeletal face.
Her teeth were eroded, her eyeballs were red.
And alone through the forest I fled.

I passed a mill on top of a hill,
And the mill was grinding white flour.
I heard a sound like clicks and pops;
Something there struck me as sour.
I peered from above at the miller's wheel;
No wheat nor grain did I see,
But femurs and skulls compressed into meal,
And one of them looked just like me
(Leaving no bone inside of my head).
And alone through the forest I fled.

At dusk I reached home, my great wooden hall,
Strong cypress ceilings and strong wooden walls
Ringed round with porches, both great and small.
Up to the front porch I started to crawl.
Alone on the porch was a rocking chair rocking,
And a baby whose naked young head was a-nodding.
I rocked him to sleep sitting back in the chair,
Running my hand through his wispy brown hair.
"Your father's come home," I wistfully said,
"Your brave father home from the forest."

The Blackbird's Heart

In the town atop the hill,
Stands a house beside a mill.
By the mill, inside the home,
Sits a cube that's made of chrome.
In this box of chrome and steel,
Spins a special silver wheel.
On the wheel, each paddle holds,
Tiny flakes of purest gold.
Pecking at the flakes so bright,
Stands a blackbird robbed of sight.
Pecking with a clicking sound,
Makes the wheel go 'round and 'round.
In the blackbird's tiny heart,
Glows a button labeled, "Start."
Press it, press it, here we go.
When you press it, blackbird crows.
When he crows, you hear this phrase:
"This is how I spend my days.
Starting my heart, spinning a wheel,
Eating gold flakes in a box of steel
In the house beside the mill,
In the town atop the hill."

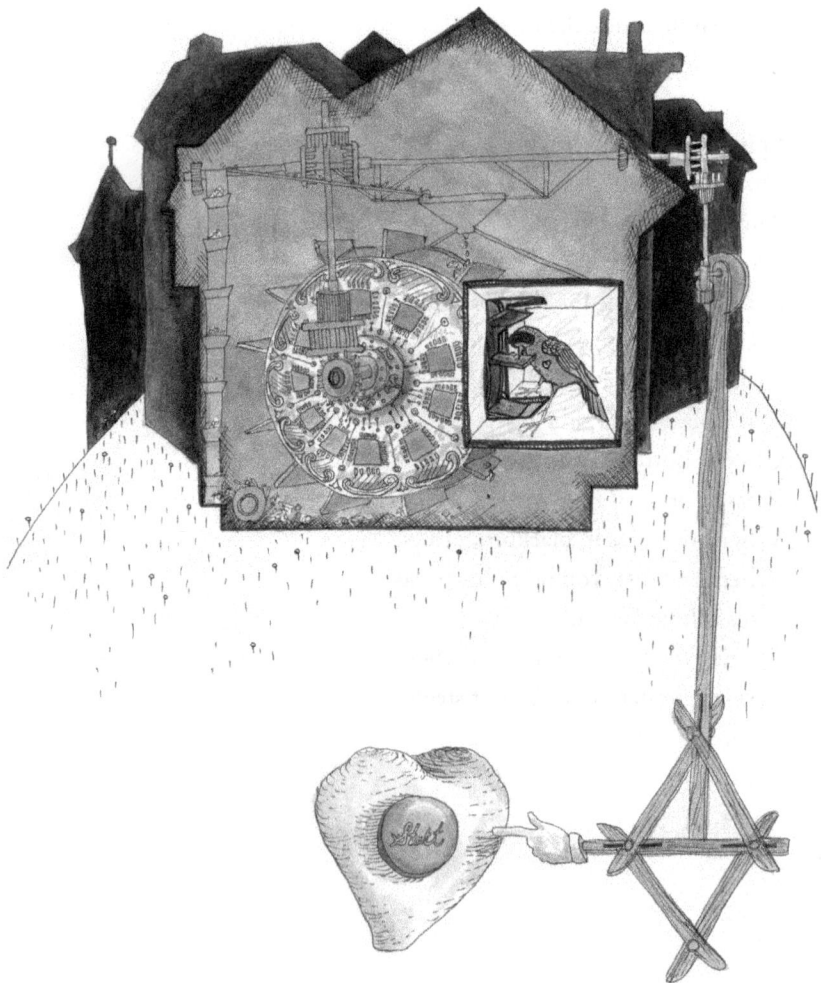

I Sent a Swallow First

I sent a swallow first, the afternoon
we met. He sang an easy song for you
in the myrtle just outside your windowsill,
and when you slept he whispered my words.
No swallow understands me now. I feel
those hearts that bat with fear inside my palm.
And when I whisper, their eyes fill with alarm.
Not even carencros come close these days
when I approach and try to grab each one.
They wheel and spin and never listen well.
Do you still hear that swallow—the one
that sang, perched on the myrtle just above your bed?
If you do, send him back and ask him
to remind me what he said.

The Marriage of the Birds

On a Monday in April, or so I have read,
A quail and a partridge prepared to be wed.

All the neighborhood birds and the neighborhood beasts
Inquired what they might bring to the feast.

The pig from the prairie showed up with his gal
And offered to bring his gal's best pal, Sal.

"Of gal friends and Sal friends we have quite enough.
It's meat for the soup that we need some more of."

Just then a crow in a bowtie flew by
With some ham and some lamb baked into a pie.

"Thank you, dear crow, but we have enough meat.
If only someone could bring bread to eat."

As if on command, a pigeon approached
With a beak full of bread and a fancy new broach.

"This bread is stone ground with the freshest of wheat.
No bread is more fine or more filling to eat."

"Of bread," said the partridge, "We're set, but I think
We could certainly use some nice wine now to drink."

As soon as these words were expelled from her beak,
A mole stumbled in and attempted to speak:

"Messieurs and mésdames, I'll have you all know,
From my cellar I've brought a tasty Merlot,

"With notes of cucumber and a hint of woodsmoke,
Aged for ten years in a barrel of oak."

"As far as fine wine, we're perfect, I'd say!
All we need now is a fiddler to play."

"You called," said a rat with a handsome mustache
And curly black hair tied up with a sash.

"I'd be happy to help and will play all night long,
If you promise no cat will consume me mid-song."

"Oh, rat, don't be silly, there's no cat around.
Now strike up a tune and let's hear how you sound."

But nobody knew that the cat was concealed
Right above in the rafters while the rat played his reel,

Until he leapt down and pounced into sight
And gulped up that musical rat in one bite.

"Meow, meow, meow," the cat purred, "all I can say,
Is I'm sorry for crashing your lovely soirée."

Around by the Wrist

New Year's has come and New Year's has gone,
Fireworks littered all over the lawn.
I fell into love with a girl in the ring
And it's oh what a beautiful morning.

I needed a girl for the first New Year's dance,
A girl who would jump, a girl who would prance.
I needed a girl who would wait for the dawn,
And it's oh what a beautiful morning.

We fell into love but we only kissed
And clumsily twisted around by the wrist.
I looked up and saw that her ribbons were torn,
But oh what a beautiful morning.

Dance with me now in the ashes of dawn.
All of the grown-ups are sleeping or gone.
Even the rooster is nodding his head,
But oh what a beautiful morning.

Father January

Gather, children, gather near—
There's a tale you all should hear.
Christmastime has come and gone.
Santa Claus has traveled on.
You've been good. You've been nice.
We haven't had to tell you twice.

Why, though, you might ask,
Now that Christmas day has passed,
Must I still be nice and good?
Must I do the things I should?

Must I still be kind today,
With Santa heading the other way?

Let me tell you so you'll know:
Yes, Santa's off for the land of snow,
But there's another man, I hear,
Who comes around this time of year.
Pale and thin with stringy hair,
He does not laugh. He only stares.
He's not jolly. He's just scary.
His name is Father January.

You've heard of a grouch. You've heard of a grinch.
You've heard of old ladies who like to pinch.
Father January's worse.
He's just like Santa, but in reverse.

When the Christmas party's through,
He keeps a peeping eye on you,
And if you do not share your toys
With the other girls and boys,

Or if you're suddenly mean and mad,
Or greedy or grumbly or just plain bad,
He'll come when you're sleeping on New Year's Eve
And shovel your presents up into his sleeve.
All of those toys you'd been waiting for,
Vanished with nothing but ash on the floor.

Therefore, children, try to remember,
Here at the end of this chilly December:
Though Christmastime has come and gone,
And Santa Claus has traveled on,
Keep being good, keep being nice.
Never make your parents tell you twice.

Claude Martin's Last Requests

We stayed at sea for seven months
And never spied the coast,
Seven sons of New Scotland,
Eating rats on toast.

The British came and burned our towns,
Defiled our virgin girls.
We fled into the forest,
Lived on nuts and squirrels.

They caught us on a winter night.
They locked us in a barn,
Shipped us out with the morning tide
Straight into a brewing storm.

When seven months had come and gone,
No food left in the hold.
The only meat left was our own,
However lean and cold.

Who would die to save us all?
The shortest straw would say.
Who would die that we might eat
And live another day?

Claude Martin drew the shortest straw,
The shortest of the seven.
He had one wish before he died
And his soul rose up to heaven.

"Let me climb the mast, my friends,
And gaze out toward the West,
One last chance to see the shore
And reach the land at last."

Up he rose into the rigging
And hooked onto the mast.
"I see!" he shouted. "I see," he gasped,
"I see the land at last."

"I see three angels in the distance,
Three angels on the shore."
We laughed to hear this raving fool.
We whet our blades some more.

But as the sun descended slowly,
Three white doves appeared.
When Claude Martin reached the deck,
We knew that land was near.

Now Claude Martin is a farmer
On a Spanish grant.
On a forty-arpent tract,
He plows his rows and plants.

One wish he has that all here know,
That all here must abide,
One wish Claude Martin asks of us,
On the day Claude Martin dies.

"Brand two crosses on my feet,
Brand them deep and red.
Before you lay me in the ground,
Be sure that I am dead.

"Be sure that I am gone, my friends,
Be sure that I am dead.
Brand two crosses on my feet,
Brand them deep and red."

Let Him Reach Heaven Dressed All in White

May he reach heaven dressed all in white
And sing when the sun can decipher his song.
When he dies, let him die right.

Over the field, three angels ignite.
Three fiery swords, three moving throngs.
Lead him to heaven dressed all in white.

With raiments arrayed at the foothills of night,
He'll open the book in sight of the dawn.
When he dies, let him die right.

Gods of the mountain rejoicing in might,
Uttering flames this short summer long.
Let him reach heaven dressed all in white.

Who can explain this musical light?
Death cannot blot out the twelve trumpets' song.
When he dies, let him die right.

Only the sun can describe this new sight,
While we rest here and tarry this season.
Let him reach heaven dressed all in white.
When he dies, let him die right.

A Benediction for Rosalie

I wrote this poem when you were young
And a toy dinosaur was your best friend.
Every night, I put my ear to your lungs
To hear when you would breathe again.
I was a wretch at playing pretend.
(Seeing you there seemed story enough.)
I tended to sit back and listen,
Your mother much better at that sort of stuff.
But once, on a New Year's Day,
In the midst of a primeval forest,
You were a triceratops,
And I, a tyrannosaurus.
We battled over a primordial turf.
You charged, and I snarled.
Our warfare shook the innocent earth,
And all creatures fled our fearsome quarrel.
Then, suddenly, the fighting stopped;
We realized we were friends.
We danced a frolicking dinosaur dance
And then we stopped and fought again.
Fighting and dancing, fighting and dancing,
Eons ago when the world was new.
A father no good at playing pretend,
Doing what he could to dance with you.

Under the Gardenia

Beneath a white gardenia
A dreamless boy slept.
Three princesses rode by
And off their horses leapt.

The oldest princess of the three
Whispered in his ear,
"Arise, arise, young shepherd boy,
The queen-to-be is here."

She poked him in his ribs
And pinched his naked calf.
He blushed and stood, saluting.
(The other sisters laughed.)

"I know you, handsome shepherd boy.
Your father is my vassal.
I'd like you to come home with us
To my own father's castle.

"Our rooms are on the upper floor,
High atop his keep.
Come and spend the night.
At the side of the princess you'll sleep."

When those words emerged
From the princess' curling mouth,
The shepherd boy fell over,
Crumpled into a crouch.

Mouth full of a white froth,
Eyes engorged with blood,
He tumbled into the roadway
And died there in the mud.

"Toll the bells," his mother yelled,
"Bow the fiddle, sound the drum.
Ring the bells all day and night,
Ring them for my son."

"Where will he be buried?
Where will his young body sleep?"
"Bury him outside the churchyard
Beneath the fleur-de-lys."

After three days of mourning,
A knock came on the door.
The sight she saw filled her with joy,
Then seized her with dread to the core.

Standing there in the dark,
Her son swayed, covered in dirt,
Face as pale as the moon above,
Blood all over his shirt.

"Mother, Mother, I've returned,
Mother, let me in.
I died three days to save my soul,
To save my soul from sin.

"Mother, Mother, I've come home
From three days down below.
I died to preserve my honor,
To save my immortal soul."

A Paper of Pins

If this is the way that friendship begins,
with demands for a gift or a crown
or trinkets, or toys—then I'll look around
and try to find you a paper of pins.
If this is the way that wondering ends,
with a little white dog, splayed on the ground
who gnaws and paws at something he found,
I'll bring him a pillow lined with white satin. I'll
imagine coffers full of gold and then
recall the key—its clinking, cold sound.
No, then? A promenade around the grounds,
A wordless walk around the bend?
Under the oak, a word of farewell,
Certainly never to see you again.

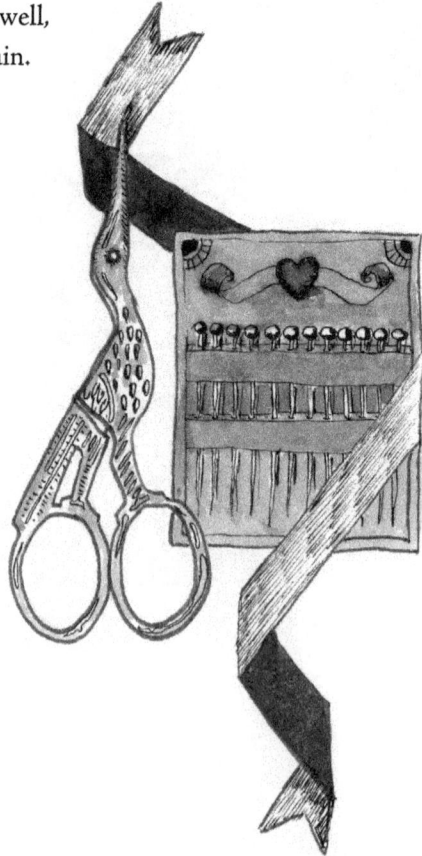

Captain Russel

Captain Russel has a house
With neither beams nor rafters,
Suitable for nesting birds.
His life is a disaster.

Captain Russel has three sons.
One's a worthless thief,
One cannot connect the dots,
One is drunk on grief.

Captain Russel has three girls
Named Janette, Jane, and Joan.
Half their time is spent in bed,
The rest spent on the phone.

Captain Russel has three steeds,
The joys of his old age.
Two have legs as thin as reeds,
And one has wooden pegs.

Captain Russel owns a goat
Whose name is Colonel Bly.
They sit sometimes and chew the cud
And watch the clouds go by.

Captain Russel has a field
Filled with bulgur wheat.
He can quickly jump across it
With one bounding leap.

But don't despair for Captain Russel.
No pity does he need.
He's happy in his foolishness.
A good old boy indeed.

The Shepherdess Queen

As I went out one evening fair,
Yonder to the forest riding,
A shepherdess with coal black hair
Beside a stream her flock was guiding.

As I approached I heard her cry,
On the wind her voice careening,
"Young prince, do not ride by.
The wolves that killed my lambs are fleeing.

"Three wolves came down and stole my sheep,
Three wolves with yellow teeth a-gnashing.
They stole three lambs, and here I weep
While they disappear into the forest crashing."

Now I, being young and full of sap,
A king's son hot with pride and vigor,
Demanded what reward I'd have,
What gifts she might deliver.

"I have no wealth in coin of gold,
No cups of shining silver,
But mittens wove from fine lambs' wool
I could most certainly deliver."

"I'll have no mittens made of wool,
No goblets wrought in silver.
I need no wealth in coin of gold.
This is what I'd rather:

"For each dead wolf I'll have a gift,
Three gifts in all that you might give.
For now the night draws quickly on
And I assume you wish to live.

"For one dead wolf, I'll take that cross
That dangles on your bosom white;
For two, I'll have a kiss from you.
For three, I'll stay the night."

And with these words, she wept again,
While I lit a glowing fire;
"If you slay these three black wolves,
You'll have what you desire."

Straight to the wood, I rode just then,
To seek the beasts and claim my treats.
I found them huddled in a foul den,
Feasting on the young lambs' meat.

I slaughtered one, my arrow straight
Puncturing his stomach.
The second beast engorged my blade.
I split him groin to gullet.

The third wolf latched onto my thigh,
But soon he knew his blunder.
I ripped out both his cursed eyes
And tore his jaws asunder.

Then I skinned the bloody hides
Of grizzled wolf and sheep.
I rode back to the shepherdess
To claim my prize and sleep.

When I returned and saw her there,
Tending the little fire,
Glittering cross and coal black hair,
I took what I desired.

And now, my people, greet your queen.
Kneel, and show your love.
For she will rule here at my side
Though she be of peasant blood.

The Crow and the Swallow

The crow and the swallow set out one day,
A lovely morning in the month of May.
Though linked by friendship and occupation,
They differed broadly in intention.
The swallow, you see, was a servant of Love,
Decreed by the gods in the heavens above
To serve as a steward for amorous souls,
To encourage affection, to make the heart whole.
When grief-stricken queen, or princess, or daughter,
High in a tower or down by the water
Despaired to discover some truth to her lover,
The swallow would swoop from the tree and recover
Those thoughts and those truths and those trembling words
And relay at once all the things he had heard
To an imprisoned prince or a sorry swain bawling.
That was his mission. That was his calling.

The crow, however, plied a somewhat different trade.
His song was unlike the swallow's sweet serenade.
While the swallow conveyed words of romance,
The crow perched alone in a hickory branch.
In a quite rapid rhythm and tones most declarative,
The crow was the master of nonsensical narrative.
When travelers passed through the hickory grove,
You wouldn't believe the lies that crow told.
"Listen up," he'd command, and tell a tall tale
About a giant ant or a minuscule whale,
A fish that could walk or a dog that could talk
Or a snake that could fly on the wings of a hawk.
Sometimes he'd boast and the nonsense would flow
From his beak. He would speak and his eyes they would
Glow: "I was born in a dust storm just west of El Paso.
My mother's a bullwhip, my father's a lasso.

I'm faster than sin and I'll tell you, my friend:
Sometimes I start before I begin,
And sometimes I stop before I am done;
And one time I tried to fight the sun.
That silly sun, he ran away in fright,
And that is why we have a thing called Night.
Then I fought the moon, and he ran away,
And that is why we have a thing called Day."

This is the sort of thing that Crow would say.
But on that lovely morning in the month of May,
The crow and the swallow conspired to trade.
The swallow would relinquish his soft serenade
And the crow would become the heart-herald divine,
A minister flying through love's crooked sky.
But when they enacted their cunning scheme,
The outcome was not what it would have seemed.
In fact, what happened was rather strange—
Not a thing changed.
No shepherd balked, no princess wept or yelled
Or seemed confounded by Crow's rhetorical spell.
In fact, to them, he made perfect sense,
Sitting there squawking on the fence.
They kissed his beak and stroked his feathers black
And begged him to take a message back.
In much the same way, the swallow failed
To spellbind travelers with true love's tales.
Indeed, they seemed as baffled as before.
He made less sense than a locked door.
"What can it mean?" Swallow asked Crow.
"What does this say about all that we know?"
"I can't explain it," old Crow replied,
"All that I know is it punctures my pride.
No one has ever made sense of my discourse,

But lovers just casually take it in stride."
So they sat there and babbled and brayed
At the end of that odd unadventurous day,
A swallow and crow, conversing in the breeze,
As twilight slipped slowly into the trees.

The Poet Begs for Charity

The Long Lent is coming. You know this
by the riders arrayed on the prairie
in the half-light. By the ring of children
locking arms, laughing, awaiting the rhyme,
by the counterclockwise circle forming
in the hidden clearing beyond the fields
and the swallows flying by the thousand
in a whorl above the cypress grove,
singing to no one but themselves.
You know somehow that things will soon begin.
Of all the masked performers, you are one,
walking softly in the dew of the ditch,
along the line all the way to the front.
You pass them all as they mill in the mud.
(Darby Hicks leading a small bleating lamb,
Sweet Mary Moreau dressed as the Boatman,
The brothers Féraille as three drummer boys,
and Elizabeth Jane from Baltimore,
Wearing red ribbons and a black *capuchon*.)
The time, the time, the time has come.
The fiddler arrives and you form the ring.
Someone has to start the song,
and that is why you sing.

Notes

A LETTER TO PIERRE GROUILLET

Many traditional French songs echo with imagery and plot related
to forgotten rural customs. One such custom is the charivari, the
carnivalesque, *courir*-like ritual of noise making and bride kid-
napping (and occasionally chicken stealing) that preceded certain
unions deemed dubious by local communities. I try to tap into some
of those ideas here, combining motifs, characters, and images from a
few different songs dealing with the contingencies of matrimony—
as well as with ritual efforts to enchant those contingencies.

THE FEUFOLLET OF IRISH BEND

The eponymous Irish Bend—a deep curve, almost a loop, in the
Bayou Têche named for the Irish who settled there in the early
1800s—has always inspired me. Its center is a deep, old, and near-
impenetrable forest, from which flows the muddy Yokely Bayou. As
Caffery family lore has it, three brothers arrived on the Bend, hav-
ing made their way from Natchez and Nashville, and the Louisiana
Cafferys descend from two of those brothers. In this poem, I try
to imagine what might have become of the third, with the help of
a bit of shared Irish/French folk belief and a tricky but rewarding
rhyme scheme courtesy of Poe. Incidentally, Poe visited the area and

stayed at the home of his former classmate Francis Dubose Richardson, whose daughter, Bethia, married the son of one of the Caffery settlers.

SAINT CATHERINE AND THE CHERUBIM

Songs about the travails of Saint Barbara (though she is usually called St. Catherine in these songs) were found in most francophone song repertories in Louisiana—not surprisingly, given the Franco-Catholic character of the region. Although often sung to a cheerful melody with chirping onomatopoeic refrains, a rather graphically violent story lies at the heart of the legend. Folk song is sometimes imagined as an antidote to or refuge from the impurities of mass media—to violence, or sex, or venality, for instance. Long before the advent of widespread literacy and mass-mediated violence, however, folklore was full of the fleshly side of life. In other words, even in songs about the holy saints of Christendom, we should not be surprised to encounter graphic violence, terrifying angels, or the Lord knows what.

SANS-SOUCI

The notion of the "enfant sans-souci," the carefree youth who becomes a superannuated hedonist, extends at least as far as the Middle Ages and the *sociétés joyeuses*—singing societies of well-off young men who composed and performed a smorgasbord of comical musical fare, often in conjunction with carnival festivities. Songs about such characters moved between oral and print culture, often via the Caveaus—eighteenth- and nineteenth-century descendants of the *sociétés joyeuses*—and their massive song collection, *La clé du Caveau*. Despite the venerability of this song type and the character at the root of it, I would venture to say that we all know someone like the speaker here, and perhaps we even envy his hardheaded yet liberated approach to life.

TÊCHE

I have a weakness for concrete poems, particularly the masterpieces of the great poet, parson, and proverb collector George Herbert. For most of my life, I have lived at one or another house on the banks of Bayou Têche, though I wrote this poem while living for a year in Washington, D.C. No one really knows where the word *Têche* comes from, but local legend links it to a Native American word for "snake," and some (notably Avery Island archivist Shane Bernard) have suggested that it may also have meant "worm." The "worm-track" patterns of Chitimacha baskets certainly resemble the shape of the Têche from above. Either way, I try to capture my own emotional tie to the muddy and lovely bayou in this poem, with a metaphysical nod to George Herbert at the end.

THE RING AND THE CORMORANT

Most famous as Louisiana French songster Blind Uncle Gaspard's (and later, Feufollet's) poignant "Sur le bord de l'eau," *La fille aux chansons* is a cycle of traditional songs in which a maiden, strolling at the water's edge, falls under the spell of a singing mariner— usually the youngest of a group of thirty or three. After she is lured aboard his vessel, things inevitably turn awry, with the girl losing her virginity (or, symbolically, her ring) or the young mariner drowning in search of her ring, or both. I use these basic narrative threads but improvise a new ending.

SUNFISH AND LOOM

The famous old song about a beloved girl who shapeshifts in order to escape unwanted advances, not unlike the dryads or naiads of the Classical tradition, is full of wisdom about lust, identity, and un-requited love. Named, like Ovid's famed anthology of such stories, "Les Métamorphoses," the song is widely attested in oral tradition in French North America in general and French Louisiana in particular, where it was recorded from the singing of Marie Pellerin and roving Cajun balladeer Edius Naquin. Preserving the dialogic form of the song, I switch the setting for a Louisiana idyll.

THE WOODEN LEG

Life gives you lemons, you make lemonade. Life gives you a wooden leg, you save some money, stay warm in the winter, and tame your wife. This amusing fabliau has been circulating back and forth between oral and print culture for a few hundred years, and my written version, based on a performance recorded in New Iberia in 1934, marks the latest episode in that cycle.

THE FLAME AND THE TOWER

The French tradition teems with songs of jealous fathers, lovelorn maidens, and the towers in which the former imprison the latter. Echoing the tale of Hero and Leander and recorded in Louisiana by John Lomax, Harry Oster, and others, the French song about a flame of love, suicidal tendencies, and blood-induced resuscitation reminds us that such things captured the adolescent imagination long before the contemporary vampire craze.

THE LOUP-GAROU

One of the more visible celebrities of Louisiana French folklore, the Loup-Garou (sometimes, Rougarou) is essentially a cross between a werewolf and chupacabra. It struck me that there were no substantial poetic attempts to summon this curious creature. The name casts an onomatopoeic spell, I think, which may partially account for the creature's longevity and popularity in Louisiana lore. I try to delve into that spell a bit here.

Proverbs and sayings, in their mother tongue, never fail to take advantage of the poetic resources of language. They are often rhythmic or alliterative, and this helps us remember and savor them. The gnomic gems of Poor Richard are the famous case in point. These important features often vanish, however, in translation. In these two pieces, I provide metrical settings for various words of Louisiana wisdom.

GABRIEL AND MADELINE

Various, relatively modern songs in Cajun French deal with the antics of mischievous godparents. Others involve situational rural romantic comedy that recalls the spirit of the fabliau. Before the car parked on lover's lane, in other words, cotton rows and henhouses fit the bill.

THE GIANTESS BRIDE

Superficial definitions of tradition imagine it to be inherently patriarchal or conservative. In truth, tradition can be both conservative and transgressive, depending on the interests of tradition bearers and their own creative impulses. Tradition, in other words, engulfs patriarchy or matriarchy, which are its poppets. "Le Petit Mari," the song concerning a disappointed wife wed to a comically miniature husband, was once sung widely in French Louisiana. In telling the tale of the beleaguered and minimized groom, I try to add another layer of perspective to the story.

HOME FROM THE FOREST

One of the attractions of working with formulaic songs like this one concerning a comically frightened woodland traveler is that the writer has a bed or a rhythm over which to encounter and explore the song's psychological core. For me, at least, the structure and the progression of the song open up that door. Here, my inhabitation of the form and the speaker's anxious mindset helped unfold my own concerns about fatherhood and mortality.

THE BLACKBIRD'S HEART

This is my take on an old cycle of enumerative narratives found widely in folk rhyme and song in Louisiana oral tradition. I love how the nested imagery runs the inner eye through its paces. I wrote this on a snowy winter afternoon far north of my normal habitat after a day chained to a computer.

I SENT A SWALLOW FIRST

Birds, usually swallows, were the social messengers of French folksong. Things have changed, of course, and the imaginary has become a digital reality, but the need for instantaneous, seemingly airborne, conveyance of desire is nothing new.

THE MARRIAGE OF THE BIRDS

I wrote this poem one morning after having spent the previous evening reading to my daughter from Dr. Seuss. His penchant for all things anapestic (boom-boom-chick, boom-boom-chick, boom-boom-chick, boom) seems to have made its mark. The poem essentially retells a well-known French traditional song performed by, among others, New Iberia/Indian Bayou singer Julien Hoffpauir, who no doubt sang it for his own daughters.

AROUND BY THE WRIST

This little poem derives from a bilingual ring game lyric sung by Lunéda Comeaux of New Iberia in 1934. In that song, the speaker reflects on the happenings at a dance on New Year's Eve the night before—a time associated in rural Louisiana French folklore (not to mention in American mass culture) with love and, particularly, kissing. Comeaux's performance evokes a kind of wistful, exhausted happiness that I try to capture here. Like the song, the poem can be sung to the melody of "Skip to my Lou, my Darling," itself best known as a ring game song.

FATHER JANUARY

I thought it time someone wrote a poem about the anti-Santa still preserved in the folklore of south Louisiana, particularly in St. Martinville, New Iberia, and the environs of Loreauville. Père Janvier, Pa Janvier, or Petit Bonhomme Janvier, in one way or another, captures a darker side of the Christmas season, as does his female counterpart, Madame Grands Doigts (Madame Long Fingers). These characters, I think, balance out the purely benevolent, corpulent Santa of the contemporary American imagination, whose own pre-American history is, of course, considerably more diabolical, or at least conflicted, than we are generally led to believe.

CLAUDE MARTIN'S LAST REQUESTS

Well known in the French oral repertoire of North America, the song about cannibalism and self-sacrifice on the open sea is even more ubiquitous in the song bag of Portugal and its colonies. Known as "A nau Catrineta," it remains popular to this day in Brazil, where it is often accompanied by a dramatic dance. Although no direct evidence suggests that this song made its way to Louisiana from the Acadian settlements of New France, my retelling takes place within that historical frame. I also draw on family lore surrounding my ancestor Claude Martin—the first Acadian settler in the area that came to be known as Breaux Bridge—and his phobia about being buried alive.

LET HIM REACH HEAVEN DRESSED ALL IN WHITE

Despite their divergent origins, the villanelle and the African American spiritual share a number of poetic traits—among them, a privileging of the hypnotic refrain, an inclination toward the esoteric and the symbolic, and a clear note of didacticism. In this poem, I build a villanelle around an idea and image I first encountered in a spiritual recorded from Albert Bradford and Becky Elzy, who sang it before the Civil War in the small church at Avery Island.

A BENEDICTION FOR ROSALIE

At rural French weddings, it was customary for fathers of the bride to sing doleful benediction songs about the imminent departure of their daughters. These songs were meant to evoke emotion and, when possible, tears. In this poem, I tried to imagine what I might say or sing to my own daughter at such a gathering in an undisclosed future. I can't speak for my audience, but I certainly ended up making myself a tearsome mess in writing this.

UNDER THE GARDENIA

Princesses, we all know, are not always nice, though they often appear to incarnate the nice and the good in French folksong. Roving captains and princes, on the other hand, are often emblems, either satirically or not, of masculine prerogative, particularly in the French *pastourelle* tradition. In this poem, I once again play with the gender roles of a widespread old song as a way of opening up the simmering psychodrama at the root of the genre.

A PAPER OF PINS

A well-known song in both the English and French North American folksong repertory, as well as in popular music courtesy of Marty Robbins and Marilyn Monroe, "Papier d'épingles" deals, on one level, with the role of gift giving in romantic relationships. When sewing and handcrafts were more a part of daily life than they are today, a "paper of pins" stood for something of little value—and thus a most worthless gift.

CAPTAIN RUSSEL

This poem is a retelling of the well-known comic song about Cadet Roussel. The song originated in the historical figure Guillaume Roussel, a hapless French bailiff who tried to improve his modest home by adding a loggia in 1780. The French populace apparently found this to be so utterly ridiculous that the song about his antics immediately "went viral" in oral tradition. Hundreds of years later, somewhat hilariously, people are still laughing.

THE SHEPHERDESS QUEEN

In the typical French *pastourelle*, whether literary or oral, a knight (or prince, or cavalier) encounters a lovely shepherdess in a rural setting. He then tries to seduce her, with varying degrees of success. Any number of things happen after the knight's initial attempt. Various bargains (sometimes subtly erotic, sometimes nakedly so) may be struck, or the shepherdess may fend off her suitor with witty wordplay. Oftentimes, these songs end in the forest on an ambiguous note. Here, I try to supply a more concrete conclusion.

THE CROW AND THE SWALLOW

In this poem, yet another involving birds, I juxtapose the amorous messenger of the traditional French song bag with the oracular crow of African American song lore. How might their poetic discourses differ, and what does this reveal about their underlying missions?

My inspiration for this poem was Seamus Heaney's "Personal Helicon," the last poem in his first book of poetry. In that poem, he creates a lush conceit for his poetic project from a bucolic childhood pastime. I try to do something similar here, working with a native conceit from bucolic Louisiana festivity.

www.ingramcontent.com/pod-product-compliance
Lightning Source LLC
Chambersburg PA
CBHW031452270326
41930CB00007B/970